BENDI BENSON SCHRAMBACH

EYES
TO
SEE

BIBLE STUDY

SEEING GOD IN THE "ORDINARY"

Published by BookBaby

7905 North Route 130

Pennsauken, NJ 08110

www.bookbaby.com

All Scripture quotations, unless otherwise indicated, are from the New International Version (NIV) copyright © 1985, 1995, 2002,2008,2011 by Biblica, Inc. Used by permission of Zondervan. All rights reserved worldwide. www.zondervan.com

Author photo by Ashley Caitlin Photography

ISBN: 978-1-09833-284-6

Printed in the United States of America

CONTENTS

INTRODUCTION

Sweet Sister-in-Christ,

I am so thankful that you are joining me for this eight-week companion Bible study to *Eyes to See: Experiencing the Wonders of God in All of
Life's Seasons.* I am convinced that the Lord desires to bless us with a bigger
picture of Him and his love for us. *Eyes to See Bible Study* aims to do just
that! Digging deeper into themes raised in the companion text, this study
invites us to press in to the One who knows us by name. My prayer is that,
as you work through these chapters over the next several weeks, you will be
strengthened and encouraged in your walk with the Lord.

In order for our "eyes to see" all that the Lord has for us, we need to
be in his Word, need to be among his people. So while you can certainly
undertake this Bible study alone, I hope that you will find other women to
join you on your journey. Proverbs 27:17 reminds us that, "As iron sharpens
iron, so one person sharpens another." In my experience, women's groups
can have a significant impact on the life and health of both women and their
families. We encourage each other. We challenge each other. We intercede
for each other. We love on each other.

And who of us couldn't use a little more of these good things?

1

If you are leading a group of ladies, it is important to set a few ground rules for your time together. Here are some that you might consider:

- **Confidentiality.** In order for us to feel safe to share intimate details of our lives, we need to know that what we say will remain confidential. Ask the women to vow to maintain the confidences of the others in the group.

- **Candor and vulnerability.** Satan does his best work when we are isolated, when we feel alone. But when we bring our cares and fears and temptations into the light, we can better see them for what they really are: struggles common to us all this side of Glory. When we allow ourselves to be candid and vulnerable, we find that we are not alone in the fight. We recruit, moreover, sister-warriors to join us in the trenches.

- **Appropriate sharing.** Some of us like to share *a lot*. Others prefer to remain quiet. If one woman is constantly dominating, it might be appropriate to gently remind her—before or after the gathering—that the goal is for all to be heard. Ideally, all of us will contribute during any one session. We all have perspectives and insights worth sharing. Indeed, the silent types should know that when they don't participate, the rest of us feel like we are the only ones with issues!

- **Avoid counseling.** If you or another woman has a suggestion for someone, invite her to coffee or lunch! Do not, however, offer guidance or counsel during the time devoted to studying God's Word.

- **Prayer.** I encourage you to allow time at the end for prayer requests and a closing prayer. As leaders, commit to praying for the ladies throughout the week and invite the other participants to do the same!

To promote intimacy and vulnerability, you may want to ask the ladies to limit the subject of their prayer requests to themselves and their nucleus families. In this way, we not only see God's hand move through our collective prayers, but—via the privileged act of praying for our spiritual sisters—we are knit together in faith and in love.

Eyes to See Bible Study is broken into eight weeks, each of which reflects on one or more chapters of the book, *Eyes to See: Experiencing God's Wonders in All of Life's Seasons.* You may want to complete the questions before gathering with other ladies. Alternatively, you may choose to talk and work through the chapter when you meet together. Certain topics or passages may speak to you more than others. Use the questions and referenced verses as jumping off points for conversation or meditation. Personalize your experience in order to best suit your needs.

The goal, of course, is to make your time in this study count for the Kingdom. My prayer is that you *will be blessed* with a greater vision of God and his love for you. I am honored to accompany you on the journey.

With affection,

Bendi

WEEK 1: BIBLICAL PROPHECY

Week 1 reflects on the chapters
"Adoption," "Of Eunuchs and Freshmen Rejoicing,"
and "Sweet Mercy."

The first few chapter of *Eyes to See* relate my conversion to Christianity at the age of 18. Though the Father was, the Bible reveals, drawing me to Himself,[1] for me, it felt like a deliberate, reasoned decision. The date and circumstances surrounding my commitment to Christ are forever etched in my memory.

Many are fortunate to be raised in a Christian home. For them, it is often an easy and natural progression to take on the faith modeled for them—however imperfectly—by their parents.

Yet all of us have a story of how God drew—or is drawing—us to Him. Our testimonies are one way to share our faith with others. Even more importantly, they are a means of giving Him glory.

Write out the following verses:

- *1 Chronicles 16:8*

- *Daniel 4:2*

- *Psalm 107:2*

- *Mark 5:19*

In *Eyes to See,* I write about the faith of Jay and Joan, who moved to a different state and began the process of adoption because of the Lord's prompting. I record the dedicated evangelism of Michael, who met with me weekly to study the Bible and answer my questions about Christianity. These servants of God, along with my discovery of some intriguing prophecies in the Old Testament and the Lord's kind wooing of my heart, ultimately led me to the faith.

What is your testimony? Are you prepared to share it? Following are some questions to help inspire you.

What was your first impression of Christianity?

Did you have family members who were Christian?

What Christian mentors influenced you?

When did you first feel the Lord tugging at your heart?

> **Our testimonies are a means**
> **of giving God glory.**
> **We are called to share them.**

"Of Eunuchs and Freshmen Rejoicing" relates my first encounter with biblical prophecy. Reading through the book of Isaiah in an introduction to the Old Testament course, I recognized what appeared to be the foretelling of Christ.

Read Isaiah 53:5-6 and make note of any details that seem to point to Jesus.

What, in the passage from Isaiah, is fulfilled in the following New Testament Scriptures?

- *John 19:34, Mark 15:17-18*

- *Mark 14:53-65*

- *1 John 2:2, Galatians 3:13*

I read *a lot* of the Old Testament during that first semester in college. From creation to Noah to Abraham and Moses, I learned the history of God's people. Yet because of my ignorance of the faith, I failed to recognize many of the prophecies that would later be fulfilled.

Write out Isaiah 46:9-10.

According to these verses, what does biblical prophecy reveal?

Prophecies fulfilled provide evidence of God's sovereignty. Demonstrating God's omnipotence throughout history, prophecies fulfilled should bolster the faith of believers.

And while prophecy alone may not be enough to win over skeptics to the faith, it certainly can pique the interest of those seeking Him.

> *Prophecies fulfilled provide evidence of God's sovereignty... They should bolster the faith of believers.*

Hundreds of biblical prophecies have already come to pass. There is historical record to substantiate it. The people and events are verifiable.

Look up the following verses and note what is predicted.

- *Isaiah 39:5-6*

- *Jeremiah 25:11*

- *Isaiah 44:24-28*

- *Isaiah 45:1-4*

All this is now documented history. Israel and Judah fell to King Nebuchadnezzar of Babylon, just as Isaiah predicted. The Jewish people were exiled to Babylon for 70 years, just as Jeremiah foretold. Then, Cyrus the Great of Persia conquered Babylon and allowed the Jews to return to Israel to rebuild the temple, just as Isaiah prophesied.

Here is the crazy thing: the books of Jeremiah and Isaiah were written 50-150 years *before* these events took place! These Old Testament prophets predicted not only the fall of Israel and Judah, but the approximate length of Jews' exile in Babylon—and even the *name* of the king who would allow the Jews to rebuild the temple in Jerusalem.

This is better than any Houdini trick. Announcing the rise and fall of kingdoms, the dates, and even the *named* actors *centuries* before they occurred is nothing short of supernatural.

Look up the following verses. What details of Jesus' life and death are foretold in these Old Testament Scriptures?

- *Psalm 16:10 and Psalm 49:15*

- *Isaiah 7:14*

- *Isaiah 6:9-10*

- *Jeremiah 31:15*

All of these prophecies were written at least 500 years before Christ. Five hundred years. That's twice as long as the United States has existed!

How do biblical prophecies—those fulfilled and those yet to come—impact your faith?

The more we study the Bible, the more irresistible it becomes. We grow in our understanding of God and his holiness. We see prophecies fulfilled, promises kept.

We see the omnipotent, mighty hand of God.

This reminds me of a quote from the book *Prince Caspian* by C.S. Lewis. It is a scene in which the young Lucy encounters the mighty Lion, Aslan, symbol of Christ, after a season apart.

"Aslan," said Lucy, "you're bigger."

"That is because you are older, little one," answered he.

"Not because you are?"

11

"I am not. But every year you grow, you will find me bigger."

> *"Every year you grow, you will*
> *find me bigger."*
> -*Aslan* (Prince Caspian)

As *we* grow in our faith, we will find *Him* bigger. We will catch an ever-greater vision of how big and mighty and awe-inspiring... *He* really is.

But we must work to grow up in our faith.

Growth as a Christian does not happen simply via the passing of time. An hour church service could never counterbalance the hours we spend each week interacting with other fallen human beings and consuming (secular) movies, television, news, and social media.

For believing in Jesus is not enough. James 2:19 says that even the Devil believes—and shudders. For us to be effective for the Kingdom of God, we need to grow up in our faith.

Daniel is a mighty example of someone who sought to know God. When taken into exile by King Nebuchadnezzar, Daniel chose not to defile himself by becoming like the Babylonians. Instead, he determined to follow after God with his whole heart.

Look up the following verses. What practices did Daniel do in contrast to those around him? How did he endeavor to press in to the God of Israel?

- *Daniel 1:3-8*

- *Daniel 6:1-16*

And the Lord blessed Daniel immensely! God granted Daniel the ability to interpret dreams. He protected him in the lion's den. He enabled Daniel to prophesy future events and sent angel messengers to enlighten to him.

Wouldn't you want to have an eternal impact on the Kingdom like Daniel? I sure would! Such things don't occur by happenstance.

As with our relationships, our health, and our work, we must be proactive in our walk with God. To grow up in our faith, we must be in his Word, the Bible. We must gather with other believers to encourage and sharpen each other. And barring unusual circumstances and seasons of life, we must serve in some capacity at our local church.

These efforts, and the revelations granted by the Holy Spirit, will help our *eyes to see* just how big—ever bigger!—our God is.

Press in, Friend! He is worth it.

> *For God to get bigger,*
> *WE need to grow in our knowledge of Him.*

As we conclude the lesson this week, consider how you might better press in to your faith this season. What is something you could do increase your vision of Him this week?

Conclude with a prayer asking the Lord to continue to open your eyes to his hand in your life. Record your prayer, below.

WEEK 2: SUBMITTING TO CHRIST'S LORDSHIP

Week 2 reflects on the chapter
"Submission."

Fallen is the state of our humanity. Since Adam and Eve in the Garden, we all wrestle with sin.

For some of us, it is addiction. For others, lust. Some contend with pride or dishonesty or unforgiveness.... But we all grapple with something.

Against what sin or sins do you struggle or have you struggled in the past?

One recurring shortcoming of mine is selfishness. In my desire to accomplish, to do, to achieve, I sometimes neglect or discount those around me. It becomes *all.about.me.*

The chapter "Submission" relates an incident that highlights this tendency. As a young wife and mother, I was faced with the choice of putting the desires and well-being of my husband over my own inclinations. I was convinced that it was "my turn."

> *There are no "turns" in Christianity.*
> *Rather, there are opportunities to*
> *demonstrate love of a sacrificial kind*

But there are no "turns" in Christianity. (Nor should there be in marriage.) Rather, there are *opportunities* to demonstrate love of a sacrificial kind.

Like Jesus did.

Paul admonishes this attitude in his letter to the church at Philippi.

Read Philippians 2:1-8.

I love Paul's soft-handed approach: *'If* you are thankful for your salvation, *then* be like Christ—humble, selfless, obedient to God.' If you are *not* thankful for your salvation, well then, no worries....

I don't know about you, but—without the Lord—I would most certainly be a mess.

I am so very thankful for my salvation.

According to Paul's reasoning, then, I must (endeavor to) emulate my Savior.

Write out Philippians 2:3-4.

These verses stand out to me. Value others above myself? Is that humanly possible? I mean, I would sacrifice for my children and, on most days, for my husband. But value the postal clerk above myself? Value the person honking in the car behind me above myself? Value the neighbor who plucks lilac blooms from our yard without asking above myself?

It isn't humanly possible.

Yet it is *divinely* possible—if we stay connected to the Vine.[1]

Several years ago, I was blessed to do the Bible study *Freedom for Mothers* by Denise Glenn.[2] Denise uses the imagery of John 15 to encourage mothers, whose sacred trust is to guide and disciple and love and discipline their indefatigable children, to draw from the Source of all that is good.

> *In order to love and serve our families and the body of Christ, we must stay connected to the Vine.*

Read John 15:1-8. What is God revealing to you in these verses?

Glenn's admonishment to *stay connected to the Vine,* Source of all fruitfulness, has stuck with me through the years—and not only while raising my children. People are fallen. Relationships are taxing. Marriage involves compromise. Children require patience. Work entails toil....

But, to mix a metaphor, God's well is never empty. There is plenty of love and joy and peace and patience and kindness and gentleness... and *selflessness,* if only I stay connected to the Source. D.L. Moody provides the following encouragement: "We are leaky vessels, and we have to keep right under the fountain all the time to keep full of Christ... What we want is a fresh supply, a fresh anointing and fresh power, and if we seek it, and seek it with all our hearts, we will obtain it."[3]

In this as elsewhere, our gracious God does not ask us to do what He has not already done. Just before the Last Supper, Jesus, Lord of the universe, modeled servanthood for his disciples.

Read John 13:1-17. Had you been at the table with the disciples, how do you think that you would have responded to this act of servility?

Reading this passage this morning, I noticed something that I had never seen before. (The Lord is kind that way.) John writes, "Jesus knew that the Father had put all things under his power, and that he had come from God and was returning to God; *so* he got up from the meal, took off his outer clothing, and wrapped a towel around his waist" (emphasis, mine). Does that look like a logical conjunction to you: 'Jesus knew who He was and where He was going, *so* He disrobed to wash some dirty feet'?

I did a little research to dig a bit more into this passage and found this in the *IVP New Testament Commentary.*

Jesus' own awareness is also an important part of the context of the footwashing. He *knew that the Father had put all things under his power* (literally, "into his hands") *and that he had come from God and was returning to God* (v.3). Here... is the description of Jesus' identity in his relation to the Father. This knowledge does not simply give Jesus the security to wash the disciples' feet—his sharing in the divine essence is what leads him to wash their feet. Jesus said that he only does what he sees the Father doing (5:19), and this footwashing is not said to be an exception to that rule. John's introduction to the event ensures that we understand God's glory is revealed in Jesus in this sign. This is what God himself is like—he washes feet, even the feet of the one who will betray him![4]

Divinity washes feet. God's glory revealed in service.

Holy are you, Lord!

I'll have to try to remember that when it's time for me to do the dishes.

God's economy is so different from our own. Christianity is full of paradoxes.

Look up the following verses and note the paradox of each.

- *Matthew 20:16*

- *2 Corinthians 12:9-11*

- *Matthew 23:11*

Did you catch that last one? Instead of resenting, groaning, complaining, or resisting the call to serve, we must remember the example of our Savior who "did not come to be served, but to serve."[5]

> "God's glory is revealed in Jesus in [footwashing].
> This is what God himself is like—he washes feet,
> even the feet of the one who will betray him!"

How terribly humbling. I'm ashamed to admit that such is not always the posture of my heart. "This is what God himself is like—He washes feet." Who am I to think that I'm too good to do the same?

Me. A sinner. "Too good" to act like God (through service).

Help me, Lord. Change my heart.

Write out Romans 12:1.

What does it mean to be a living sacrifice? Alexander Maclaren offers this explanation:

The metaphor of sacrifice runs through the whole of the phraseology of [the] text. The word rendered "present" is a technical expression for the sacerdotal action of offering. A tacit contrast is drawn between the sacrificial ritual... and the true Christian sacrifice and service. In the former a large portion of the sacrifices consisted of animals which were slain. Ours is to be "a living sacrifice".... These other sacrifices were purely outward, and derived no efficacy from the disposition of the worshipper. Our sacrifice, though the material of the offering be corporeal, is the act of the inner man, and so is called "rational" rather than "reasonable".... The last word of [the] text, "service," retains the sacerdotal allusion, because it does not mean the service of a slave or domestic, but that of a priest. And so the sum of the whole is that the master-word for the outward life of a Christian is sacrifice. That, again, includes two things—self-surrender and surrender to God.[6]

Self-surrender. Surrender to God. Sacrifice. This is the Christian way.

Consider the relationships that you (may) have with the following people. What would it look like to share God's love with them through service or sacrifice?

- *an unpleasant colleague at work*
- *a neighbor*
- *your mother/mother-in-law*
- *your husband*

These things are not easy, friend. But we can do it!

Consider them opportunities to worship the Lord.

**Self-surrender. Surrender to God. Sacrifice.
This is the Christian way.**

Read Matthew 25:31-46.

Complete verse 40:
The King will reply, "Truly I tell you, whatever
_____ *for one of the least of these brothers*
and sisters of mine, _____.*"*

In the greatest act of love the world has ever known, the Lord of the universe stepped down from heaven—not to be worshiped, not to receive our praise, not to bask in the glow of his glory, but—to *serve* humanity.

The creator of Heaven and Earth chose to *submit*—not to his appetite, not to his good pleasure, but—to the Father's will.

And He calls us to do likewise.

Write out the following Scriptures.

- *Galatians 5:13*

- *1 Peter 4:10*

- *1 Peter 1:15-16*

> *In the greatest act of love the world has ever known, the Lord of the universe stepped down from heaven— not to be worshiped, not to receive our praise, not to bask in the glow of his glory... but to serve humanity.*

God calls us to holiness. And holiness compels surrender to the Father. Oh, that our flesh would not get in the way of growing more like our Savior in this area of sacrifice!

Have you surrendered to Jesus? He stands at the door and knocks.[7] If you have never confessed Jesus as Lord, I invite you to submit to Him today. It only takes a confession of your fallen nature, an acknowledgement of your need for Him, and your willingness to put Him on the throne of your life. Romans 10:9 states: "If you declare with your mouth, 'Jesus is Lord,' and believe in your heart that God raised him from the dead, you will be saved."

If you do invite Jesus into your heart today, or if you have questions and would like to talk about it further, let me know! (You can reach me through my website.) I would love to celebrate with you and with the angels, sweet Sister in Christ.

For those of you who have prayed the prayer of salvation, in what area do you find it difficult to submit to the Christ's Lordship during this season? Pray that God would soften your heart and give you his perspective on the matter.

WEEK 3: THE POWER OF WORDS

Week 3 reflects on the chapters
"Deception," "Tree of Life," and "Fireworks in Heaven."

Several chapters of *Eyes to See* allude to the importance of our speech. "Deception," for example, shares an incident in which words, used deceitfully, harm relationship. "Tree of Life," on the contrary, relates an event in which encouraging words have a positive impact. And "Fireworks in Heaven" narrates the salvific power of the Christian declaration of faith.

The Lord emphasizes the significance of speech throughout the Bible.

Look up the following Scriptures and make note of the impact of the uttered words.

- *Genesis 1:3, 1:6, 1:9, 1:11, 1:14, 1:20, 1:24, 1:26*

- *Genesis 17:1-5, 32:22-28*

- *Matthew 8:5-13*

God literally *spoke* creation into existence. He renamed Abram and Jacob to better reflect the reality of their lives (present and future). And the Lord used words (and faith)—in the case of the centurion and others—to heal.

These are God's utterances. Divine speech acts imbued with supernatural power. A God of miracles accomplishing the miraculous via the spoken word.

Yet the Bible reveals that *human* utterances are also of consequence. What we say matters—to God and to others.

Look up the following Scriptures and make note of the import of human speech.

- *Genesis 27:1-40*

- *Matthew 16:13-20*

- *Matthew 12:30-37*

These are some pretty weighty verses. Irrevocable blessings. Divine revelations. The unmasking of the human heart. *All this by the voicing of a few words!*

As Christians, our speech merits some consideration. That July 4th when our daughter accepted Christ into her heart was my very favorite Independence Day. Though I had wanted to skip church to take care of "important" preparations for our afternoon guests, when Emily announced that she had made a decision for Christ at Sunday School I was acutely reminded of what *really* matters: a relationship with God—now and in Eternity.

It is not enough to *believe* Christ. We must *profess* Christ. We do this, first, with our tongues.

> *Irrevocable blessings. Divine revelations. The unmasking of the human heart. All this by the voicing of a few words!*

Complete the following verses.

- *Romans 10:9-10. If you* _____,
  *"Jesus is Lord," and believe in your heart that God raised him from the dead, you will be saved. For it is with your heart that you believe and are justified, and it is*_____

  _____.

- *1 Corinthians 12:3. ...no one*
  _____ *except by the*
  Holy Spirit.

A holy mystery.

Another biblical axiom about the power of words is highlighted in the chapter "Tree of Life." There, I relate an incident that occurred in my university classroom. A student on the autism spectrum, fearful at the prospect of having to present her work in front of her classmates, found the courage to complete the assignment *because of the verbal encouragement of her peers.*

Complete the following verses.

Proverbs 12:18: The words of the reckless pierce like swords, but

_____.

Proverbs 15:4a: The soothing tongue is _____ ...

Healing. Life. What beautiful imagery.

The tree of life is referenced as early as Genesis 2. It was in the Garden along with the tree of the knowledge of good and evil. Explicating this biblical reference, Randy Alcorn writes: "In Eden, the tree [of life] appears to have been a source of ongoing physical life. The presence of the tree of life suggests a supernatural provision of life as Adam and Eve ate the fruit their

Creator provided. Adam and Eve were designed to live forever, but to do so they likely needed to eat from the tree of life." Alcorn posits that the tree, moved—at the Fall—from Eden to Paradise, will be relocated to the New Earth when Christ returns.[1]

> *Gentle words are a tree of life;*
> *a deceitful tongue crushes the spirit.*
> *-Proverbs 15:4 (NLT)*

Consider for a moment this metaphor. The Bible likens a "soothing" ("wholesome" [NKJV] ,"gentle" [ESV]) tongue to *a tree of life*. What the Creator of the universe placed in Eden as supernatural provision for his children is analogized, in this proverb, to *our speech*.

Think of it! We—via a soothing, gentle "tongue"—can provide emotional and spiritual nourishment to another human soul with the words we speak. It is an astonishing assertion.

What power we wield with our tongue!

Write out Ephesians 4:29.

As Christians, we are called to be attentive to our speech. Why is it, then, that we often speak so carelessly? Vulgarities, insults, flippant remarks... they neither honor God nor edify our fellow humans.

Think back to a time when you were hurt by the words of others. How did this speech act mark you?

> *Why is it that we often speak so carelessly?*
> *Vulgarities, insults, flippant remarks... they neither*
> *honor God nor edify our fellow humans.*

Mom taught me a rhyme to help assuage the pain of unkind words: "Sticks and stones may break my bones but words will never hurt me." And while I tried to believe it as a child, it wasn't true. Words do hurt. Indeed, the pain they inflict is often more enduring than that of physical injury.

God knows this. Which is why the Bible admonishes us so strongly to wield our words with care.

Complete the following verses.

- *Proverbs 15:4: The soothing tongue is a tree of life,*
  but _____.

- *Proverbs 17:20: One whose heart is corrupt does not prosper;*
  _____.

Is it the perverse tongue (of Proverbs 17:20) that causes the trouble? More likely, it is trouble that follows those with perverse tongues. This is to say that our speech habits are really a reflection of our character.

Let that sink in.

We'll return to it a bit later.

In another example of the unruly nature of the tongue, the chapter, "Deception," tells the story of the first time our son lied to me. For this first-time mother, the event was nothing short of devastating. In *Eyes to See*, I draw an analogy between this lie and the first lie of Adam. Genesis 3 reads:

> Then the man and his wife heard the sound of the Lord God as
> he was walking in the garden in the cool of the day, and they

hid from the Lord God among the trees of the garden. But the Lord God called to the man, "Where are you?"

He answered, "I heard you in the garden, and I was afraid because I was naked, so I hid."

And he said, "Who told you that you were naked? Have you eaten from the tree that I commanded you not to eat from?"

The man said, "The woman you put here with me—she gave me some fruit from the tree, and I ate it."

Avoidance, omission, deflection... all are forms of deception. All are sin, resulting in broken fellowship with God and others.

So much for "soothing," "wholesome" and "gentle."

Read James 3:1-12. What stands out to you in these verses?

Lying is just one manner that we sin with words. What are others—mentioned or not mentioned in this passage from James?

Avoidance, omission, deflection... all are forms of deception. All are sin, resulting in broken fellowship with God and with others.

In his commentary on James 3, Pastor David Guzik identifies several ways that we "stumble in word."

> We stumble in word about ourselves with our boasting, exaggeration, and selective reporting.
>
> We stumble in word about others with our criticism, gossip, slander, cruelty, two-facedness, and anger; or with flattery and insincere words meant to gain favor.[2]

"To not stumble in word," Guzik summizes, "shows true spiritual maturity."

If it's not too much to ask, sweet Sister, how are you doing in this area of your Christian walk? What are some ways that you could improve your use of the tongue?

Prudence is in order. Temperance. Restraint.

Is this why there are so many verses that suggest the wisdom of *not* talking? Egad! Less of my own voice?! Where would the world be without my blather? Better off, apparently.

Complete the following verses.

- *James 1:19: My dear brothers and sisters, take note of this: Everyone should be _____ and slow to become angry.*

- *Proverbs 10:19: Sin is not ended by multiplying words,*
  _____.

- *Proverbs 11:12:* _____ ,
  but the one who has understanding holds their tongue.

- *Proverbs 21:23:* _____
  keep themselves from calamity.

> **Our speech habits expose our intemperance. For while talking, I can't reflect deeply. I can't listen to others. And I certainly can't hear the voice of God. Much talk reveals a lack of self-restraint.**

Who knew that that Bible had so much to say about keeping our mouths shut?! I know that, had I heeded this advice, I certainly could have avoided some calamities along the way.

How about you?

Not only that, but our speech habits expose our intemperance. For while talking, I can't *reflect* deeply. I can't *listen* to others. And I certainly can't hear the voice of God.

Much talk reveals a lack of self-restraint.

It is in this light that we better see the correlation between our speech and our spiritual health. This psalm of David illustrates it well.

Lord, who may dwell in your sacred tent? Who may live on your holy mountain? The one whose walk is blameless, who does what is righteous, *who speaks the truth* from their heart; *whose tongue utters no slander*, who does no wrong to a neighbor, and *casts no slur on others*; who despises a vile person but honors those who fear the Lord; who keeps an oath even when it hurts, and does not change their mind; who lends money to the poor without interest; who does not accept a bribe against the innocent. Whoever does these things will never be shaken (emphasis, mine).[3]

A self-disciplined tongue = one whose walk is "blameless."

(I'm having a strong sense of James 3 déjà vu right now. You?)

Write out James 3:2

We might show self-restraint while eating. We might demonstrate willpower at the gym. We might even exhibit single-mindedness in our study of God's Word. But if we can't stop our tongues from wagging, there is something awry in our Christian walk.

We will never be perfect this side of Heaven. Still, *this should be our aim.* The Bible's many admonitions on this subject are important reminders that I, for one, have progress to make in the area of taming the tongue.

You?

Let's let the Lord be Lord. Even of our tongues.

You are not alone in this fight, friend! Let's close today by praying that the Holy Spirit would reveal speech tendencies that need refining in us. Let's pray, too, for the power to change.

WEEK 4: THE HOLY SPIRIT

Week 4 reflects on the chapter
"Benny and the Border Collie."

"Benny and the Border Collie" relates an experience I had at a prophetic conference. Following a time of worship and an exhortation from the pulpit, I received what I interpreted as a personal word of encouragement. This incident spurs my belief to this day.

A singular facet of our faith is the mystery. Yes, there are good and rational arguments for the existence of God. But these can neither account for the virgin birth nor explain the resurrection of the dead. And what is a levelheaded person to make of a Spirit that lives inside we who profess Christ?

This week we will investigate the Third Person of the Trinity: the Holy Spirit. He is, in fact, mentioned quite early in Scripture.

Read Genesis 1:1-3.

How would you describe the Spirit's role in this passage (see also Job 33:4 and Psalm 104:30)?

So God the Father was not alone "In the beginning." According to the *NIV Study Bible,* the Spirit was also "active in creation, and his creative power continues today."[1]

According to John 1:1-5 and Colossians 1:15-16, who else was there, "In the beginning"?

Three in one. A divine enigma. The Trinity is one of those things that we will not fully understand this side of Glory. It's one of those things that reminds us that He is God and we are not.

> *Three in one. A divine enigma. The Trinity is one of those things that we will not fully understand this side of Glory. It's one of those things that reminds us that He is God and we are not.*

I find it fascinating that "creative" is a quality associated with the Spirit. And surprising. Had I been asked before my investigation to write a list of adjectives to describe the Holy Ghost, "creative" would not have figured on it.

What words would you use to describe the Holy Spirit?

Yet creative is definitely one of the Spirit's attributes. This characteristic is highlighted in yet other passages of the Bible.

Read Exodus 31:1-5 and 35:30-33. What words are associated with the Spirit in this story?

What tasks will Bezalel undertake?

As one artistically challenged, I am heartened by the creative nature of the Holy Spirit. But, on second thought, not so surprised. To create is to form, to beget, to shape. And isn't that what the Spirit does in us when we submit our lives to Christ's Lordship? We are changed, shaped... *transformed* by the Spirit of God.

What do the following verses reveal about the Holy Spirit's role in the life of the believer?

- *John 3:1-8*

- *John 16:8-11*

- *I Corinthians 12:13*

- *Galatians 5:16, 22-23*

- *Titus 3:5*

> **To create is to form, to beget, to shape. And isn't that what the Spirit does in us when we submit our lives to Christ's Lordship? We are changed, shaped... transformed by the Spirit of God.**

Thus, while unseeable, the Spirit is not imperceptible. He affects believers in real, tangible ways. Spiritual rebirth, conviction of sin, belonging in the Church, godly lives, a new nature... The Holy Spirit transforms us from the inside. He works to conform us to the image of Christ. Pretty miraculous stuff!

The Spirit manifests Himself in other ways as well.

What evidence of the Spirit do we read about in Numbers 11:23-30 and 24:1-5?

The Holy Spirit is also associated with prophecy. You might remember that in Week 1, we looked at several Old Testament prophecies fulfilled in the New.

Yet biblical prophecy is not always about *fore*telling. It is sometimes about *forth*telling. Stan Jantz explains: "Even in the Old Testament times, the prophets of God spent most of their time relaying God's message of repentance and hope to his people. Revealing God's future plans was not the biggest part of their jobs as prophets."[3] Like those who were "cut to the heart" by the message of Peter, filled with the Holy Spirit on the day of Pentecost,[4] we sometimes just need a bold call to act (or, in that case, repent).

The Apostle Paul outlines the proper use of prophecy and other gifts bestowed by the Spirit in his letters to the churches in Rome and Corinth.

What gifts of the Holy Spirit are mentioned in Romans 12:3-8 and I Corinthians 12:1-11?

Full disclosure: thoughtful and earnest believers disagree on the interpretation of these passages. In particular, they hold differing views on the continued existence of these gifts in their supernatural manifestations. The three positions are, in a nutshell, these. Cessationists believe that the spiritual gifts outlined in Romans 12 and I Corinthians 12 ended with the death of the last living apostle. This view originated during the Reformation and is most associated with the Reformed tradition. Continuationists believe that these gifts continue into the present day. This position is historically linked with the Catholic, Methodist, and Pentecostal churches. A third, in-between position is made up of those "open but cautious" to the continued existence of spiritual gifts of the supernatural kind.

For what it's worth, I find myself in the camp of those "open but cautious" to continuationism. For while I believe in a God of miracles, the fallen nature of humanity and the real existence of religious charlatans oblige prudence. I arrived at this position through both the study of Scripture and personal experience. The faith granted to Jay and Joan to move their family to a new state resulting—providentially—in their ability to help someone in need and draw me to the Lord in the process is but one example.[5]

How did the Spirit direct Philip in Acts 8:26-29, 39?

The Holy Spirit said to Philip, "Go over and walk along beside the carriage."
-Acts 8:29 (NLT)

Dear Sister-in-Christ, I would encourage you to continue to seek wisdom from the Lord in this area, with the knowledge that *this is not a salvation issue.* Like the choice of worship music, carpet color, and service times, on this topic we can amicably disagree.

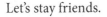

Let's stay friends.

What are your thoughts about this subject?

Are you familiar with your church's position?

What is the reason for the gifts of the Spirit according to I Corinthians 12:7?

"The common good" here is the good of the Church. Spiritual gifts—earthly or supernatural—are not intended for our own personal glory. Neither are they purposed for our emotional ecstasy. They are, instead, tools for building up the body of Christ.

Unfortunately, we sometimes pervert what was intended for God's glory. What R.A. Torrey bemoaned nearly 100 years ago persists today.

There are many Christians who in seeking the baptism with the Spirit are seeking personal ecstasy and rapture. They go to conventions and conferences for the deepening of the Christian life and come back and tell what a wonderful blessing they have received, referring to some new ecstasy that has come into the heart, but when you watch them, it is difficult to see that they are any more useful to their pastors of their churches than they were before, and one is compelled to think that whatever they have received, they have not received the real baptism with the Holy Spirit.

Ecstasies and raptures are all right in their places. When they come, thank God for them... but in a world such as we live in today, where sin and self-righteousness and unbelief are so triumphant, where there is such an awful tide of men ,women, and young people sweeping on toward eternal perdition, I would rather go through my whole life and never have one touch of ecstasy but have power to witness for Christ and win others for Christ and thus save them than to have raptures 365 days in the year but no power to stem the awful tide of sin, to bring men, women, and children to a saving knowledge of my Lord and Savior Jesus Christ.[6]

A sense of God's presence is a blessing for the believer, to be sure. But the Christian walk is not supposed to be a never-ending summer camp. So-called "Spirit Only" believers tend to focus on their feelings, "believing God is speaking to them through their thoughts and impressions, which leaves the door open to selfish desires."[7] Alternatively, "Word Only" believers focus exclusively on God's word; they "have more of a tendency toward legalism, proudly avoiding certain sins while failing to show love and mercy to others."[8]

We need the Word of God, yes. We also need the Spirit of God. *Let's be people of both.*

What are your tendencies in this area?

How can you better aspire toward both?

Paul devotes a lot of ink to the *unity* of the Church. Interestingly enough, both Romans 12 and I Corinthians 12 (the passages about the gifts of the Holy Spirit) elaborate on this theme. To the Romans, Paul writes: "just as each of us has one body with many members, and these members do not all have the same function, so in Christ we, though many, form one body, and each member belongs to all the others."[9] The metaphor of a body reminds us that, as believers, we belong to each other; the gifts of the Spirit are intended to serve the whole. Paul uses similar language in his letter to the Corinthians: "we were all baptized by one Spirit so as to form one body—whether Jews or Gentiles, slave or free."[10]

One Spirit. It marks us as believers.

> *"Doctrine explains who the Holy Spirit is. The next step is to fellowship with and experience the Holy Spirit in ways that cannot be explained in human terms." -A. W. Tozer*

Write out the following verses:

- *1 Corinthians 6:19*

- *Romans 15:13*

- *Romans 8:14*

What does it mean to be *led* by the Spirit? How do we do this? We can't see Him. No audible voice directs our course.

The Bible tells us that the Holy Spirit is a Person. Jesus calls him our Advocate, Counselor or Helper[11] and even promises that the Spirit will "teach us."[12] This, of course, is only possible if we are listening, if we are interacting with Him, engaging Him in "conversation." A.W. Tozer writes, "Doctrine explains *who* the Holy Spirit is. The next step is to fellowship with and experience the Holy Spirit in ways that cannot be explained in human terms."[13] We must know Him. Not just know *about* Him.

But "fellowship with" and "experience" the Holy Spirit? How?

Torrey suggests the following: "We are... to recognize His presence, His gracious and glorious indwelling, and give to Him complete control of the house He already inhabits, and strive so to live as not to grieve this holy one, this divine guest."[14] In concrete terms: we might acknowledge the Holy Spirit in our prayers. We should welcome Him into our devotional time. We can worship Him in our songs of praise and thanksgiving. We are to surrender to his work in our lives.

> **Let us be people of the Word**
> **AND**
> **people of the Spirit.**

Read I Thessalonians 5:16-22. What do you think that Paul meant by "quench the Spirit"?

Torrey's remarks (above) reference yet another letter of Paul.

According to Ephesians 4:29-32, how do we "grieve" the Holy Spirit?

(Did you notice the speech thing again? Or is the Holy Spirit just convicting my heart in this area? *Sheesh!*)

Sealed with the Holy Spirit. That is an amazing thought. Unlike the prophets of the Old Testament, New Testament believers receive this gift once and for all.

Yet receiving Him is only the beginning. As with all aspects of our Christian faith, we are to grow in it. In so doing, we cultivate the fruit of the Spirit outlined in Galatians 5—the love, joy, peace, patience, kindness, goodness, faithfulness, gentleness and self-control.

Who wouldn't want this bounty?

I certainly do. The Lord is glorified in this. And it is all about Him.

And because Jesus came to seek and save the lost,[15] it is, by extension, about them. Souls are at stake. Jantz sums it up well: "The Holy Spirit's function in the life of the believer is to help us become spiritually minded in everything we do so that two things will happen: We will see the world from God's perspective, and the world will see God's perspective in us."[16]

> *"The Holy Spirit's function in the life of the believer is to help us become spiritually minded in everything we do so that... we will see the world from God's perspective, and the world will see God's perspective in us." -Stan Jantz*

Let's allow the Holy Spirit to continue to enlighten us on God's perspective. He wants to give us eyes to see. (The book *Eyes to See,* is, in effect, my effort to communicate a glimpse of spiritual reality that I have perceived in my life.) Let us be amenable to the Spirit so that the world might see God's perspective in us.

Friend, what is your next step with the person of the Holy Spirit? Invite Him—even now—into a time of prayer. Ask Him to lead you in a greater understanding of Himself. Record what He reveals to you, below.

WEEK 5: TRUSTING GOD WITH WHAT WE CANNOT CONTROL

Week 5 reflects on the chapters
"Vocations," "Poetic Provision," and "Nurture and Nature."

In *Eyes to See: Experiencing God's Wonders in All of Life's Seasons,* I share several stories that betray my struggle to release to the Lord that which I felt had been entrusted to me. In "Vocations," it was our daughter and her future aspirations. In "Nurture and Nature," it was our son as he transitioned to his new residence in a faraway state.

Truth be told, I spent many years "arm-wrestling" with God about our children. I prayed for his favor, to be certain, for his protection and care. But I also prayed (begged and pleaded) for an end to certain relationships, for an opening of certain opportunities, for various and sundry details of their lives—and my husband's—in areas where I thought that I knew best.

Have you ever felt as if you were "arm-wrestling" with God? What about? What resulted from it?

The Bible actually records a wrestling match with God. The funny thing is: God's opponent was also a control freak like me.

Read Genesis 32 and use this chapter to answer the following.

- *What was Jacob's emotional state as he set out on his journey? (See verses 7 and 11.)*

- *Was this state justified? (Review Genesis 27, if needed.)*

- *What did this emotional state inspire in his relationship with God?*

- *Identify two outcomes of the wrestling match described in verses 24-31.*

Jacob is a wily character. He not only steals his brother's birthright[1] and runs away,[2] leaving the land promised to the children of Abraham,[3] but—the way I read it—Jacob appears to dictate the terms of his relationship *with God.* He does this even *after* the Lord blesses him with a vision of Himself! Genesis reads:

> Then Jacob made a vow, saying, "If God will be with me and
> will watch over me on this journey I am taking and will give
> me food to eat and clothes to wear so that I return safely to my
> father's household, then the Lord will be my God and this stone
> that I have set up as a pillar will be God's house, and of all that
> you give me I will give you a tenth."[4]

If You will be with me and feed me and clothe me and bring me safely where *I* want to go, *then* I will serve You and give you a tithe.[5] 'Tis a bit impertinent, don't you think?

And yet... how often have I done the same?

Have you ever tried to "make a deal" with God?

How did it turn out?

> *Jacob's bargain with God goes something like: "If You will be with me and feed me and clothe me and bring me safely where I want to go, then I will serve You and give you a tithe." 'Tis a bit impertinent, don't you think? And yet... how often have I done the same?*

Prior to our eldest child's departure for college, I spent a lot of time "wresting with God" about the future He had for him. One day, I felt as if the Lord answered me. (He is so gracious that way.) I recorded my conversation with God for our son in a journal that I kept for him over the years. Here is an excerpt.

> While I was praying for you this morning, I began trying to reason with the Lord. I told Him how much I was going to miss having you in my daily life. Then, realizing that He is a God of relationship, I reminded Him that He has always been able to enjoy the company of his Son—except for a couple of days when Jesus was in the tomb.
>
> So I asked Him: since I can't be with you all the days of your life, can He? And He promised that He would.
>
> And is.
>
> And will be.

Tears come to my eyes rereading this. *God is so faithful.*

The good news, friend, is that the same God who wrestled with Jacob bends his ear to hear our prayers.

Complete the following verses:

- *Psalm 116:1: I love the Lord, for* _____ _____; *he heard my cry for mercy.*

- *1 Peter 3:12: For the eyes of the Lord are on the righteous, and* _____.

- *1 John 5:14: This is the confidence we have in approaching God: that if we ask anything according to his will,* _____.

Not according to our will, mind you. According to God's will.

It was God's will to break what needed to be broken in the heart of Jacob. As Charles Spurgeon notes: "There was something that needed to be taken out of Jacob, —his strength and his craftiness; and this angel came to get it out of him." [6]

And yet Spurgeon still commends Jacob's request of a blessing: "Bravely said, O Jacob! And ye sons of Jacob, learn to say the same. You may have what you will if you can speak thus to the covenant angel, 'I will not let thee go, except thou bless me.'"

I will not let You go, unless You bless me, Lord! And bless my family, too!

What blessing do you seek from the Lord today?

Jacob's blessing was a new name. No longer would he be called Jacob, "the supplanter," but Israel: "he who struggles with God."

I must admit: I like that name. The people of Israel, the Jewish nation, the people who struggle with God.

Let us be people who struggle with God. In prayer. In petition. In inquiry. In study. Let us be people who ask for blessings.

He is able.

And then, let's leave our requests with Him. And trust that He is God.

He is God when my kid doesn't make the team. He is God when people die. He is God when my husband loses his job. He is God when a viral pandemic sweeps the earth.

He is God. And I am not.

> *"Bravely said, O Jacob! And ye sons of Jacob, learn to say the same. You may have what you will if you can speak thus to the covenant angel, 'I will not let thee go, except thou bless me.'" - Charles Spurgeon*

Write out Romans 8:28.

Do you believe this, friend? If you do, then there is no reason to keep fretting over things that you have entrusted to Him.

Yes, I know the parable of the persistent widow. And I admire her.

Read Luke 18:1-8.

Like the widow, we should "always pray and not give up." The nuance I'm trying to suggest is that we who love God and are called according to his purposes should pray and then *stop worrying*. We should pray and leave it with Him.

God is just. He wants—He *knows*—what is best for us. And He can bring it to pass. In his time.

Even if it doesn't always look how we think it will look.

I shared a beautiful example of this in the chapter entitled "Poetic Provision." Jay and Joan did not worry about how they would pay the bills when they picked up their family and moved to follow the Lord's call; they were not anxious about how they would fund their retirement years. And the Lord provided for these faithful servants. In his time.

> *And we know that in all things God works for the good of those who love him, who have been called according to his purpose. -Romans 8:28*

King David is a model of one who rested in God's promises. Though anointed by Samuel to be king, David did not attempt to overthrow King Saul. He waited for God to place him on the throne. *For.fifteen.long.years.* During much of this time, David was on the run, hunted by King Saul.

Yes, David prayed. David contended with God on this matter. Yet unlike his forefather, Jacob (abetted by mother, Rebecca), David didn't try to take matters into his own hands. He trusted that the Lord would "work all things for good" for him. And He did.

The Bible names David "a man after God's own heart."

Read Psalm 34, believed to have been written while David was running from Saul's men, and answer the following.

- *What does the psalmist advise—directly and by example—in verses 1-3?*

- *What "actions" does the Lord accomplish in verses 4 and 6?*

- *What is the role of the angels (verse 7)?*

- *What will God do for the "righteous," we who put our trust in the Lord (verses 15-19)?*

- *Do you recognize the prophecy about Jesus in this psalm? (If not, review John 19:36.)*

- *What from this psalm inspires or comforts you?*

The subject of trusting God with all that we cannot control would not be complete without mention of Paul's spirited exhortation to the church at Philippi. Keep in mind while reading this that Paul penned this missive *while in jail.*

> Rejoice in the Lord always. I will say it again: Rejoice! Let your gentleness be evident to all. The Lord is near. Do not be anxious about anything, but in every situation, by prayer and petition, with thanksgiving, present your requests to God. And the peace of God, which transcends all understanding, will guard your hearts and your minds in Christ Jesus.[7]

Rejoice. The Lord is near. Fear not! Pray. Rest in the peace that comes from knowing Him.

Interestingly enough, this formula for peace largely imitates the structure of David's psalm: praise God (Psalm 34:1-3) for He is able (Psalm 34:4-22). In this is our peace.[8]

Yes, there is great uncertainty in our world. Unforeseen changes in our personal lives.

But none of it is a surprise to the Lord of the universe.

As Christians, we must not be worry warts. We must not be control freaks. If we are to be effective witnesses for his Kingdom, we must allow God's peace to reign in our hearts. Contend with God in prayer. Believe that He hears us (*because He does!*). And abide in the peace that passes all understanding.

Sweet Sister: Is there a burden that you need to lay at the foot of the cross once and for all? Today is the day. Write out your prayer, below.

> **As Christians, we must not be worry warts. We must not be control freaks. If we are to be effective witnesses for his Kingdom, we must allow God's peace to reign in our hearts. Contend with God in prayer. Believe that He hears us (because He does!). And abide in the peace that passes all understanding.**

WEEK 6: SEEING GOD (IN THE ORDINARY)

Week 6 reflects on the chapters
"Trampolines and Umbrellas," "A Divine Appointment,"
"Preach!," "Known and Loved,"
"Waiting Tables in Nashville," and "New Life."

Several chapters (the entire book?) of *Eyes to See: Experiencing God's Wonders in All of Life's Seasons* endeavor to make the case that God is involved in even the intimate details of the lives of his people. And why wouldn't we believe this? Romans 8:28 promises as much: "And we know that *in all things* God works for the good of those who love him, who have been called according to his purpose," emphasis mine. (That one is worth committing to memory. I dare you.)

Have you ever felt like God was speaking to you through circumstances or events? Explain.

The chapter "Trampolines and Umbrellas" suggests evidence of God's working of all things to protect my marriage. While stewing over my husband's current mood and allowing myself to indulge in a sense of victimhood, God allowed me to hear the perfect song to convict my heart of its selfishness. (Pretty creative messaging, don't you think?) The Holy Spirit reminded me of the promise I had made to God and to my husband: "For better or for worse."

"A Divine Appointment" narrates how God brought into my life a soon-to-be missionary to a French-speaking land in need of a translation of the training manual, which I was able to provide. Had I volunteered at church six months later, I would have missed the blessing that it was to serve the Church during what was for me a dark season grieving my empty nest.

"Preach!" relates how the Lord convicted our son of hypocrisy (and a bit of pharisaism). After negatively judging one boy's (perceived) inaction, Alexander realized that he was, in fact, planning on doing the same thing he had accused the other boy of doing. The Holy Spirit worked to soften our son's heart.

"Known and Loved" tells the story of how God used my appreciation for the creatures of the air to bless me with a greater sense of his love for me. After accidentally hitting a small bird on my way to work, He reminded me that He, too, cares for the sparrows. How much more, then, His love for me!

"Waiting Tables in Nashville" records the casual conversation with a colleague that the Lord used to encourage our son—and us—in his new stage in life.

And "New Life" relates the answered prayers—and provision!—that allowed our daughter to lead a Christian summer camp. This opportunity blessed her with a glimpse of God's Kingdom and her place in it.

All these events could be described as circumstantial. Happenstance. Coincidence.

And yet, I know the Lord. And I have grown to recognize Him in some of the signs and wonders of my daily life.

How, you ask?

Like all good relationships, ours with God requires time. We need to get to know Him. We need to know his character. And since we cannot walk with Him and talk with Him as the disciples did, we do this primarily *through his Word.*

(I see a theme in this study. You?)

Write out the following Scriptures.

- *Isaiah 55:8*

- *2 Timothy 3:16*

- *Hebrews 4:12*

Sure, you have heard a few stories about God, maybe even think that you know what Jesus looks like (lol), but if you don't know his *thoughts* about something, don't know how He would react to something you said or did, it would be difficult to grow close. And it would be a stretch for Him to call you, as he did Moses, friend.[1]

> *"For my thoughts are not your thoughts, neither are your ways my ways," declares the Lord. -Isaiah 55:8*

Or let's reverse that. Imagine that someone found your profile on Facebook and "befriended" you. Then she direct messaged you whenever she was in trouble to ask for financial help or marital assistance or parenting advice... You would likely be taken aback since, apart from a few profile pictures, she doesn't know you from Adam.

It is a poor analogy, I know, since God is God and not a Facebook acquaintance. The Lord knows us intimately. Better than we know ourselves.

But I hope you see the point.

The thing is: we need to work on our relationship with God even more diligently than those with other humans since *God.is.not.a.mere.mortal.* He is Other.

Our main tool to accomplish this is his Word. God speaks to us through the Bible. To grow in our relationship with Him, we must make the study of Scripture our daily bread.

Write out Romans 12:2.

Renewed minds are minds that are empowered to see the hand of God all around us. And, let me tell you, it's some exciting stuff.

> *We need to work on our relationship with God even more diligently than those with other humans since God.is.not.a.mere.mortal. He is Other.*

A few years ago, I was blessed to complete Henry T. Blackaby's excellent Bible study *Experiencing God.*[2] (I highly recommend it!) A portion of the book addresses the matter of how God "speaks" to us. According to Blackaby, the Holy Spirit communicates with us by means of the Bible, prayer, circumstances, and the Church.

Eyes to See shares several examples of the Lord speaking to me through circumstances: chance meetings, providential encounters, divine appointments. My book also celebrates the wonders of creation, which can, at times, be used to speak to our hearts.

Creation is not the Creator, however.

What do the following verses remind us not to worship?

- *Deuteronomy 17:2-7*

- *Romans 1:25*

That twinkling star in the sky is not your childhood friend sending winks from Heaven. That bird lingering on the branch outside of your window is not your recently deceased grandmother (may she rest in peace). They are, instead, the Lord's majestic handiwork. They are intended to point us to Him.

What do the following verses teach about creation?

- *Psalm 19:1-4*

- *Job 12:7-10*

God is God. Creation is but his workmanship. Of this we are part.

> *For since the creation of the world God's invisible qualities— his eternal power and divine nature— have been clearly seen, being understood from what has been made, so that people are without excuse. -Romans 1:20*

Let's now consider how we might better "see God" through the practice of prayer.

When and for what reasons do you pray?

What has the Lord revealed to you through prayer?

The Bible records many prayers of God's people. I'm thinking that the Lord meant to provide some good models for us to emulate. Together, let's look at the petitions of three exemplars of the faith.

Read 1 Samuel 1 and answer the following:

- *Who prays?*

- *What is the request?*

- *Describe her emotional state while praying.*

- *Describe her emotional state after speaking with Eli (verses 18-19).*

- *How was her prayer answered?*

- *What is the Lord showing you from this example?*

Hannah's prayer reminds us that we can bring our fears, our tears, to the Lord. And, as one prone to emotion, I am thankful that the Bible does not omit her anguish. God is near in both our merriment and our misery.

Hannah's prayer also reminds us that the Lord's timing is often not our own. I don't know about you, but when I want something, I tend to want it *now.* I wonder, though, had Hannah been blessed with a child early in her marriage, would she have offered Samuel in service to the Lord? Probably not. And where would Israel have been without this amazing leader of God's people?

Hannah's prayer reminds us, finally, that the Lord can use our offerings for things greater than we can imagine. Sounds to me like yet another good reason to dedicate some of our talents and resources to the Holy One of Israel.

What is the Lord calling you to "offer" to Him in this season?

Here's another prayer for our consideration.

Read Daniel 9:1-23 and answer the following.

- *Who prays?*

- *What is the posture of his heart?*

- *Describe the content of this prayer.*

- *What is the result of his prayer?*

- *What is the Lord showing you from this example?*

> *We do not make requests of you because we are righteous,*
> *but because of your great mercy. -Daniel 9:18*

Daniel's prayer canvasses his humility before God. He acknowledges his sin and the sin of the Israelite nation that led to their captivity in Babylon.

But Daniel does not wallow in despair. Even in this prayer of repentance, he elaborates on the steadfast love and righteousness of our God. With conviction and contrition, he pleads for the Lord's mercy. And God honors Daniel with a heavenly messenger: the angel Gabriel himself.

I'd sure love to be visited by an angelic guest. You? Just one more reason to pray.

Here's our last prayer.

Read 2 Chronicles 20:1-19 and answer the following.

- *Who prays?*

- *How does he begin this prayer?*

- *What does he tell God in verses 7-11?*

- *What is the result of his prayer?*

- *What is the Lord showing you from this example?*

- *Write out the final sentence of verse 12.*

One thing I notice from these prayers is that they all begin with an acknowledgement of God's sovereignty, his power and goodness. "Lord Almighty" Hannah pleads. "Lord, the great and awesome God, who keeps his covenant of love with those who love him and keep his commandments," Daniel extols. " Lord, the God of our ancestors... You rule over all the kingdoms of the nations. Power and might are in your hand, and no one can withstand you," Jehoshaphat exalts.

With their words and in their hearts, these servants place the Lord upon his throne. His rightful place. For only when He is there do we accurately see where we are. And who we are.

He is holy. We are sinful.

He is mighty. We are weak.

He is faithful. We are prone to wander.

Such introductions should humble us. Awaken us anew to the supernatural transaction in which we partake. Beginning our prayers by acknowledging our communion with an Almighty God should help transition us from the material into the spiritual realm.

> *With their words and in their hearts, these servants place the Lord upon his throne. His rightful place. For only when He is there do we accurately see where we are. And who we are.*

Personally, I like to pray aloud while on walks. (Fortunately, I am generally accompanied by a four-legged companion so the neighbors don't think I've lost my wits.) Praying aloud keeps me on point and out of my head. It ensures that I don't lose my train of thought or fall asleep in the throne room.

What helps you in your practice of prayer?

Admittedly, I have never heard the sound of God's voice. Still, I have on occasion heard *from* Him while praying.

Sometimes, it's a novel idea. (Ask me about that sometime; it's a funny coincidence.) Other times, it's a sudden conviction. In the case of the chapter "Known and Loved," it was a new revelation.

And while the chance to hear from God is not the only reason we should pray, it can be a wonderful fringe benefit.

I'd like to close this week's study with this encouragement. In order to see God in the ordinary, *we need to look for Him.*

We look for Him, among other places, in his Word. We can see Him, according to Romans 1:20, in creation.

We seek Him (reiterating Blackaby) in prayer, in circumstances, and in the wisdom of the Church and its people.

The Bible promises that when we seek Him, we will find Him—when we seek Him with our whole heart.[3]

Open your heart, dear sister! Open your heart and your eyes to the God of miracles great and small! And enjoy the show.

What will you do to seek the Lord this week?

Pray that the Lord will open the eyes of your heart[4] to an even greater vision of Him. Record your prayer, below.

WEEK 7: WORSHIP

Week 7 reflects on the chapter
"It Is Well."

You may have guessed that the title of the chapter "It Is Well" alludes to the powerful hymn by Horatio Spafford.

What is your current favorite hymn or worship song?

But did you know that "It Is Well with my Soul," published in 1876, was written following the tragic death of Spafford's young son in 1871 in the great Chicago fire, which ruined him financially, *and* the heartbreaking death of Spafford's four daughters at sea in 1873? Such affliction. It's impossible to image.

Having endured these losses, Spafford could yet affirm God's goodness. It is... astonishing really. Grab some tissue, friends, and let's review the verses of this mighty hymn.

> When peace like a river, attendeth my way,
> When sorrows like sea billows roll;
> Whatever my lot, Thou hast taught me to say
> It is well, it is well, with my soul.
>
> Though Satan should buffet, though trials should come,
> Let this blest assurance control,
> That Christ has regarded my helpless estate,
> And hath shed His own blood for my soul.
>
> My sin, oh, the bliss of this glorious thought!
> My sin, not in part but the whole,
> Is nailed to the cross, and I bear it no more,
> Praise the Lord, praise the Lord, O my soul!
>
> For me, be it Christ, be it Christ hence to live:
> If Jordan above me shall roll,
> No pang shall be mine, for in death as in life,
> Thou wilt whisper Thy peace to my soul.
>
> But Lord, 'tis for Thee, for Thy coming we wait,
> The sky, not the grave, is our goal;
> Oh, trump of the angel! Oh, voice of the Lord!
> Blessed hope, blessed rest of my soul.
>
> And Lord, haste the day when the faith shall be sight,
> The clouds be rolled back as a scroll;
> The trump shall resound, and the Lord shall descend,
> Even so, it is well with my soul!

How did the Lord speak to your heart as you read/sang this hymn?

Kinda says it all, doesn't it? The world and its trappings are passing away. We can't take anything with us (except, I like to think, the loved ones who know the Lord).

Without Christ, we are dead in our sins—and none of us is getting out of here alive! Without Christ, our fate is eternal separation from God, weeping and gnashing of teeth.[1]

Evidently, losing everything has a way of reminding us of the crux of the matter: it is all about Jesus.

One of the best ways I have found to remind myself of this (and get over myself!) is to lift the name of the Lord in song.

Praise and worship is, in fact, one of many ways that we acknowledge Christ's lordship. Yes, we are called to obey his commandments.[2] Yes, we are to love one another.[3]

But worship is perhaps the only thing that we can give to the Lord that He has not first given to us.

> **Worship is perhaps the only thing that we can give to the Lord that He has not first given to us.**

Literally *hundreds* of verses call us to "sing" to the Lord, to "praise" Him aloud with our voices.[4] Let's consider a few.

Complete the following:

- *Psalm 9:11.* _____ *of the*
  Lord, enthroned in Zion; proclaim among the nations what he has
  done.

John Gill had this to say about this verse.

> The psalmist having determined in the strength of grace to praise the Lord himself, and show forth all his marvellous works..., here calls upon others to engage in the same work; the Lord is not only to be praised, which may be done by celebrating the perfections of his nature, and the works of his hands; by giving him thanks for mercies temporal and spiritual, and by living to his glory; but his praises are to be sung by a modulation of the voice in musical notes, as the word used signifies; see Song of Solomon 2:12, where the same word is used of the singing of birds; and this is to be done by the saints jointly, in concert together, as Paul and Silas in prison sang the praises of God; and there is great reason why they should join together in this work, since they share the blessings of divine grace in common together; and it is their duty to stir up one another to this service, as well as to other parts of worship.[5]

The psalmist exhorts us to sing of God's marvelous works. Like the birds (!!!), we are called to lift our voices in chorus, to tell of the great things that the Lord has done.

Corporate praise *encourages* the faithful. It "stirs us up" for service. Singing alongside our brothers and sisters in Christ reinforces the fact that we do not walk this path alone. I, for one, am thankful for that.

Here is another psalm admonishing worship.

Complete Psalm 150.

_____the Lord.

_____ *in his sanctuary; praise*

him in his mighty heavens.

2 *Praise him* _____;

praise him for his surpassing greatness.

3 *Praise him* _____,

praise him with the harp and lyre,

4 *praise him* _____

praise him with the strings and pipe,

5 *praise him with the clash of cymbals,*

praise him with resounding cymbals.

6 _____.

Praise the Lord.

The exhortation is clear. We are to praise the Lord. With our voices. With our instruments. With our bodies.

> **The exhortation is clear. We are to praise the Lord. With our voices. With our instruments. With our bodies.**

I have always had an interest in languages. Each unique tongue reflects, in great part, the way that its culture perceives the world. Here is a cool example. The French translation for "praise and worship" is "louange et adoration." And while "louange" basically signifies the same things in French as it does in

English (praise, words of praise, worshipful praise), "adoration" signifies not only "worship" in the Judeo-Christian sense, but an intense emotion of love.

Do you sing to the Lord as if you really love Him? Like adore *Him? Why or why not?*

I hope that I am wrong, but my sense is that *most of us* do not do this enough. I mean, I've been in several churches where half the congregants never opened their mouths. And I can only think of one church that I have attended that would even allow dancing. (Strange, since David danced before the Lord[6] and was called "a man after God's own heart."[7])

Yes, I know that we must maintain order in our worship services.[8] And I don't want to cause anyone to stumble.[9]

I'm just suggesting that we make worship, the lifting of our voices in song, the posture of our bodies and our hearts, a priority. He is worthy.

So much for the issue of obedience.

Onto the matter of faith.

Read 2 Chronicles 20:14-22 and answer the following.

- *What message does Jahaziel deliver (verses 15-17)?*

- *What is the reaction of Jehoshaphat and the people of Judah and Jerusalem (verse 18)?*

- *What is the reaction of the Levites (verse 19)?*

- *What is Jehoshaphat's war plan (verse 21)?*

- *At what moment does the Lord ambush their enemies (verse 22)?*

Is that crazy or what? The Lord could have sent the ambush at Jehoshaphat's signal. Or he could have just taken out their enemies with fire and sulfur as he did Sodom and Gomorrah. Or God could have simply sent another enemy to wipe them out.

Yet the Lord set off the ambush at the sound of their *praise*.

To be clear, David Guzik notes, "it was not their praise that won the battle, rather it was their faith; yet their praise was sure *evidence* of their faith. When one really believes the words and promises of God, they cannot but help to praise Him."[10] The Israelites lifted their voices because they *believed* that the battle was the Lord's. Their response was worship.

Do you really believe the words and promises of God?

If so, does your worship reflect it? If it doesn't, why not?

Let's turn now to a New Testament example of worshipful singing. This passage was referenced by John Gill, above.

Read Acts 16:16-34 and answer the following.

- *Why were Paul and Silas thrown in jail?*

- *What were they doing at the time of the earthquake?*

- *What was the response of the jailer?*

- *What is your guess of why the jailer had that reaction?*

Do you really believe the words and promises of God?
If so, does your worship reflect it?

On the matter of the jailer's response, my guess is that the he was surprised by the peculiar conduct of these prisoners. "Praying and singing hymns to God around midnight" were not likely behaviors generally observed in jail.

The author of Acts notes that "the other prisoners were listening to them." Evidently, the jailer was as well. And based on his response, he was attracted to the joy and peace and message of salvation that he heard in the songs and prayers of Paul and Silas.

This is yet another reason to worship: it has the potential to draw others to the faith. I distinctly remember this aspect of worship services while still deciding what I thought about Christianity. The joy that I observed on the faces—and in the musical notes—of the worshipers was definitely intriguing.

Convinced? Convicted? I hope so. But for good measure, I'll mention another consequence of worship.

Neuroscience is finally catching up to the Bible. And you know what they have discovered? (Anyone? Anyone?)

Worship is good for us. Citing the findings of several researchers, Michael Liedke enumerates some of the many health benefits evidenced in those who worship regularly. Among them:

> a significant decrease in the deleterious effects of chronic fight or flight activation and the decrease in heartrate, blood pressure, blood glucose levels and serum markers of inflammation.... measurable psychic effects, measurable decreases in depression, anxiety, chronic pain and even posttraumatic stress...[11]

Physical, mental, and psychological benefits from worshiping the Lord? Sounds like a win-win-win to me!

These gifts are, of course, *not* the reason why we worship God. (A grateful heart offering a sacrifice of praise[12] to the One who brought us from death to life is reason enough.) Such bounty is just another example of the kindness of our God who blesses us for doing what we are called to do.

What we were made to do.

In recent years, I have begun to make worship music a regular spiritual discipline. In addition to worshiping with the family of God at church, I play—and sing along to! —worship music almost every day. As in the chapter, "It Is Well," I make a deliberate point to do so when I am melancholy or distressed or just need to rouse my spirit. Like Spafford, I have come to realize that worship is good medicine for the soul.

In worship, I am reminded of who I am and whose I am.

I am reminded of his faithfulness.

I am reminded that my biggest problem is taken care of.

And I am thankful.

No ambush. No earthquake. Just a regrounding of my spirit in its ultimate purpose: to give God glory.

> *In worship, I am reminded of who I am and whose I am.*
> *I am reminded of his faithfulness. I am reminded that my*
> *biggest problem is taken care of. And I am thankful.*

Conclude this week's study by completing and meditating on the following verses.

- *Isaiah 43:21. ...the people I formed for myself that they may*

- *Psalm 95:6. Come, let us* _____
  _____, *let us*
  kneel before the Lord our Maker;

- *John 4:23. Yet a time is coming and has now come when the true*
  worshipers will worship the Father in the Spirit and in truth, for
  _____.

- *Revelation 4:11. "You are worthy, our Lord and God,* _____
  _____, *for you*
  created all things, and by your will they were created and have their
  being."

In worship, as in prayer, we engage in a supernatural communion with God. In worship, we invite his presence into our midst. Let's not miss out on experiencing Him through worship!

Fellow worshiper, let's close today by spending a few minutes lifting our voices to the Lord in song. I'll meet you in the throne room.

WEEK 8: PRACTICING GRATITUDE

Week 8 reflects on the chapters
"Miracles" and "Blessings."

Let's begin this week's study with a little Bible trivia, shall we? Match each quote with the biblical character who said it:

1. *"I know that my redeemer lives, and that in the end he will stand on the earth."*[1]

    a. *A former shepherd and fugitive of the king mocked by his own brothers*

2. *"I have learned the secret of being content in any and every situation, whether well fed or hungry, whether living in plenty or in want."*[2]

    b. *A former Pharisee jailed for his controversial religious ideas*

3. *"Who am I, Sovereign LORD, and what is my family, that you have brought me this far?"*[3]

    c. *One of Jesus' half-brothers*

4. *"Consider it pure joy, my brothers and sisters, whenever you face trials of many kinds,"*[4]

    d. *A formerly-barren woman offering her child in service to the Lord at the temple*

5. *"a servant of Jesus Christ"*[5]

    e. *A man whose children were all killed and whose fortune was destroyed.*

6. *"My heart rejoices in the Lord; in the Lord my horn is lifted high. My mouth boasts over my enemies, for I delight in your deliverance."*[6]

    f. *The head of the First-Century church in Jerusalem*

How'd you do? Did you recognize these pillars of the faith? (1.e, 2.b, 3.a, 4.f, 5.c, 6.d.)

Are you impressed with Job who, following the loss of his children and fortune, yet declared: "I know that my redeemer lives, and that in the end he will stand on the earth"?

Are you moved (as I was) thinking about Hannah, the woman who had struggled for years with infertility, who—on the occasion of delivering her only child to the temple where he would spend the rest of his life in service to the Lord—yet affirmed: "My heart rejoices in the Lord"?

Are you convicted by the fact that it was Paul who wrote the letter about being "content in all circumstances" from one of his stints *in jail?*

I am likewise inspired by the humble posture of David (3), the joyfulness of James amidst real persecution (4), and the meekness of Jesus' own half-brother, Jude (5). Considered together, I would say that this group of saints exudes not just faith and humility before their God, but gratefulness—no matter their lot and lived experience on the earth.

What are you grateful for today? List the first ten things that come to mind.

Gratefulness is, in large part, about perspective. It's about recognizing who we are— sinners made of dust yet loved and redeemed by grace—and acknowledging who He is: Lord, King, and Redeemer.

> *Gratefulness is, in large part, about perspective. It's about recognizing who we are—sinners made of dust yet loved and redeemed by grace—and acknowledging who He is: Lord, King, and Redeemer.*

I am the first to admit that my life has been blessed. (My personal hashtag is #thewomanmostblessed.) God's hand has held me through the years. He has worked all things for my good. Most days, I see it and am thankful.

Yet, on those days when allow myself to indulge in victimhood, I can find ample fodder to feed the beast. Instead of writing *Eyes to See: Experiencing God's Wonders in All of Life's Seasons,* I could have easily penned *Woe is Me: I'm Feeling Sorry for Myself.* I doubt you would have wanted to read it. (I certainly wouldn't wish to.)

Do you struggle at times with a victim or entitlement mentality? If so, what does your whining look like?

As humans, we must work at gratefulness. As believers, we are called to it.

Psalm 100, believed to have been written by Moses, exemplifies a heart full of gratitude.

Read Psalm 100 and answer the following.

- *What is first commanded (verses 1-2)?*

- *How are we described in verse 3?*

- *What are we asked to do in verse 4?*

- *What is the reasoning for this command (verse 5)?*

The psalmist directs us to give thanks *because God is good*. Because He is faithful. Spurgeon's rousing commentary on verse 4 is worth quoting at length.

> In all our public service the rendering of thanks must abound; it is like the incense of the temple, which filled the whole house with smoke. Expiatory sacrifices are ended, but those of gratitude will never be out of date. So long as we are receivers of mercy we must be givers of thanks. Mercy permits us to enter his gates; let us praise that mercy. What better subject for our thoughts in God's own house than the Lord of the house. And into his courts with praise. Into whatever court of the Lord you may enter, let your admission be the subject of praise: thanks be to God, the innermost court is now open to believers, and we enter into that which is within the veil; it is incumbent upon us that we acknowledge the high privilege by our songs. Be thankful unto him. Let the praise be in your heart as well as on your tongue, and let it all be for him to whom it all belongs.[7]

As Christians, we have great reason to rejoice: payment for our spiritual debt, direct access to the Father, eternal life... We owe all to the Lord.

I think that we lose sight of this sometimes. Indeed, I think that we *often* lose sight of this. The physical reality surrounding us clouds our vision to the spiritual reality we cannot see.

What messages does our culture promote about what we are entitled to or "deserve" in this life?

> **"So long as we are receivers of mercy we must be givers of thanks." -Charles Spurgeon**

Comfort? Health? A "perfect" husband? Obedient children? A house on the lake (lol)?

The Bible promises none of those.

What we deserve is punishment. Yet God extends mercy.

What we deserve is death. Christ died on the cross in our place.

And though nothing good lives in us,[8] the Lord of the universe deigns to call us "child."

These spiritual realities should compel thankfulness. Active thankfulness. Eternal and endless thankfulness. As believers, we are called to express this gratefulness "in our heart and on our tongue" to the Lord of hosts.

The psalmist isn't the only one to urge us in this practice.

Read 1 Thessalonians 5:12-22 and answer the following questions.

- *List 5 specific exhortations of Paul.*

- *Which one (written down by you or not) do you need to most work on currently?*

- *Which one do you think that our contemporary culture needs to hear?*

- *What difference do you note between the commands listed in verses 16,17,19,20,22 and the command about thankfulness (verse 18)?*

- *Write out the second half of verse 18.*

> *Rejoice always, pray continually, give thanks in all circumstances; for this is God's will for you in Christ Jesus. -1 Thessalonians 5:16-18*

Paul also gives instructions for living to the church in Colossae.

Read Colossians 3:12-17 and answer the following.

- *List 5 specific exhortations of Paul.*

- *Which one (written down by you or not) do you need to most work on currently?*

- *Which one do you think that our contemporary culture needs to hear?*

- *Which two verses address thankfulness?*

- *How are you doing in the area of thankfulness/gratefulness to God?*

God's will for us as believers is thankfulness.

Why do you think that is?

Might it be that thankfulness is appealing? Might it be that thankful people are pleasant companions? Might it be that grateful hearts are attractive (to unbelievers)?

I would posit that, unlike my unwritten hardship tale, *Woe Is Me,* gratefulness might be a fragrant aroma, not only—as Spurgeon suggested—to our Lord, but to those who do not yet know Christ.

And we are to be about our Father's business.

(Again, I sense a theme.)

(And here's another one.) "Coincidentally" enough, gratitude, like worship, is *good for us.* (Have I mentioned how kind the Lord is?)

According to a 2015 article by *Psychology Today,* gratitude not only improves psychological health, it has a positive impact on our physical and mental health, relationships, sleep, and self-esteem.[9]

I could definitely stand to grow in some of these areas.

You?

Let us choose[10] to be grateful for all that the Lord has done for us.

And let's endeavor to give Him glory—and draw others to the faith!
—with our thankfulness.

As we draw our study to a close, I want you to know just how thankful I am for you, Sweet Sister. Thankful for your faith. Thankful for your companionship. Thankful to walk this walk with you.

What "entitlements" do you need to lay at the foot of the cross today?

Write out a prayer of thankfulness to our gracious God. He is worthy.

ENDNOTES

Biblical Prophecy

[1] John 6:44

Submitting to Christ's Lordship

[1] See John 15.

[2] Denise Glenn. *Freedom for Mothers.* Houston, TX: Kardo International Ministries, 2009.

[3] D. L. Moody. *Secret Power.* Shawnee, KS: Gideon House, 2015. 35.

[4] "Jesus Washes His Disciples' Feet." *IVP New Testament Commentaries: John 13.* InterVarsity Press, 2020.

[5] Matthew 20:28

[6] Alexander Maclaren. "Expositions of Holy Scripture: Romans 12:1." *BibleHub.com.* 2020. biblehub.com/commentaries/maclaren/romans/12.htm

[7] Revelation 3:20

The Power of Words

[1] Randy Alcorn. "What is the Tree of Life?" *Crosswalk.com*. Salem Web Network. 2016. www.crosswalk.com/faith/bible-study/what-is-the-tree-of-life.html

[2] David Guzik. "James 3-Warnings and Words to Teachers." *Enduring Word*. 2018. enduringword.com/bible-commentary/james-3

[3] Psalm 15:3-5

The Holy Spirit

[1] *New International Version Study Bible*. Grand Rapids, MI: Zondervan, 2011. 10 n.1:2.

[2] Ibid.

[3] Stan Jantz. *Fire and Wind: Unleashing the Power and Presence of the Holy Spirit*. Eugene, OR: Harvest House, 2020. 111.

[4] Acts 2:37.

[5] I tell their story in the *Eyes to See* chapter entitled "Adoption."

[6] R.A. Torrey *The Person and Work of the Holy Spirit*. Grand Rapids, MI: Zondervan, 1974. 154-55.

[7] Jantz 89-90.

[8] Ibid.

[9] Romans 12:4-5

[10] I Corinthians 12:13.

[11] John 14:26, 15:26, 16:7.

[12] John 14:26.

[13] A.W. Tozer. *Alive in the Spirit*. Ed. James L. Snyder. Bloomington, MN: Bethany House, 2016. 30.

[14] Torrey 94.

[15] Luke 19:10.

[16] Jantz. 27.

Trusting God with What We Cannot Control

[1] Genesis 27

[2] Genesis 28

[3] Genesis 15:18-21 and Genesis 26:3

[4] Genesis 28:20-22

[5] Abraham had already established the tithe. See Genesis 14:17-20 and Hebrews 7:1-4.

[6] Spurgeon, Charles Haddon. "Commentary on Genesis 32:4." *Spurgeon's Verse Expositions of the Bible.* StudyLight, 2020. www.studylight.org/commentaries/spe/genesis-32.html.

[7] Philippians 4:4-7

[8] For a great study on Philippians about stopping negative thought patterns, see Jennie Allen's *Get Out of Your Head,* Nashville: Thomas Nelson, 2020.

Seeing God (in the Ordinary)

[1] Exodus 33:11

[2] Blackaby, Henry T., Richard Blackaby, and Claude V. King. *Experiencing God: Knowing and Doing the Will of God.* Nashville: Lifeway, 2007.

[3] Jeremiah 29:13

[4] Ephesians 1:18

Worship

[1] Matthew 8:12

[2] John 14:15

[3] John 15:12

[4] The Psalms are full of such exhortations. See, in particular, Psalms 30, 33, 47, 66, 95, 96,98, 149. See also Ephesians 5:19.

[5] Gill, John. "Commentary on Psalm 9:11." Exposition of the Whole Bible, 1763. StudyLight, 2020. www.studylight.org/commentaries/geb/psalms-9.html

[6] 2 Samuel 6:14-22.

[7] 1 Samuel 13:14

[8] 1 Corinthians 14:26-40

[9] See Romans 14:19 and 1 Corinthians 6:12.

[10] David Guzik. "2 Chronicles 20 - Jehoshaphat's Victory." *Enduring Word*. 2018. enduringword.com/bible-commentary/2-chronicles-20

[11] For but one such study, see Michael Liedke, "Neurophysiological Benefits of Worship." *Journal of Biblical Foundations of Faith and Learning* 3:1. 2018. 1-9.

[12] Hebrews 13:15

Practicing Gratitude

[1] Job 19:25

[2] Philippians 4:12

[3] 2 Samuel 7:18

[4] James 1:2

[5] Jude 1

[6] 1 Samuel 2:1

[7] Charles H. Spurgeon. "Treasury of David." *Psalm 100*. GraceGems, 2020. gracegems.org/Spurgeon/100.htm

[8] Romans 7:18

[9] Amy Morin. "7 Scientifically Proven Benefits of Gratitude." *Psychology Today,* 2015. www.psychologytoday.com/us/blog/what-mentally-strong-people-dont-do/201504/7-scientifically-proven-benefits-gratitude

[10] On this subject, I recommend once again Jennie Allen's study *Get Out of Your Head.*